To Sheila

Wishing you a very Special day
for your 60th birthday.

Just thought you may like a few reminders
of your earlier days.

Unfortunately St. Luke's School is not one
of the photos but the church is there!

Lots of Love

Janice John

Robert & Laura & of course Othello

XX

BRITAIN IN OLD PHOTOGRAPHS

NORWOOD

JOHN COULTER

SUTTON PUBLISHING

Sutton Publishing Limited
Phoenix Mill · Thrupp · Stroud
Gloucestershire · GL5 2BU

First published 2002

Title page photograph: Knight's Hill, 1909.

British Library Cataloguing in Publication Data
A catalogue record for this book is available from the British Library.

ISBN 0-7509-2919-7

Typeset in 10.5/13.5 Photina.
Typesetting and origination by
Sutton Publishing Limited.
Printed and bound in England by
J.H. Haynes & Co. Ltd, Sparkford.

CONTENTS

The south tower of the Crystal Palace dominates countless old photographs of Norwood. This was the view up Anerley Hill from Hamlet Road, *c.* 1910. The tram was passing Waldegrave Road.

INTRODUCTION

This is essentially a portrait of Norwood a hundred years ago. There are a few pictures from the 1920s and one or two from the '30s or later, but the great majority show the three suburbs as they were before the First World War. Edwardian West, Upper, and South Norwood were very different from their modern successors. Here you will find pubs and hotels, orphanages and schools, bandstands and bowling greens, and churches and vicarages that are now only fading phantoms of the memory. It was a world largely free of motor cars – I notice only half a dozen among these 200 pictures – but in ample compensation there are numerous examples of more noble forms of transport: trains, trams, horse buses, and every type of carriage and cart. Five of Norwood's railway stations are featured.

The most striking change in Norwood during the century has been the replacement of large houses by blocks of flats. It has been common to cite wartime bombing as the main cause of this. At the risk of being branded a Blitz denier I will point out that of the 1,500 or so substantial detached houses built in Norwood in the nineteenth century some 800 have been demolished; and that of those 800 14 per cent were destroyed by bombing during the Second World War, and 58 per cent by developers in the 1960s and '70s. In Croydon Norwood those two decades accounted for 67 per cent of the lost houses.

As usual, economic trends had more influence over the waves of destruction than any other forces. In the booming 1920s there were many indications that Norwood life was returning to the style that had been interrupted by the First World War. Most of the big houses continued to be singly occupied, often by the pre-war families, and there was little back development in the large gardens. This return to normal was ended abruptly by the Slump. In the early 1930s most of the big houses were converted into flats. Towards the end of the decade there was a growing trend towards demolition and redevelopment, especially in Lambeth Norwood. Only fourteen large houses disappeared during the 1920s, seventy-two in the '30s. A boom in such schemes was evident in 1938 and 1939, but all were halted by the outbreak of war, and only resumed, if at all, in the 1950s.

The comparative poverty of Britain in the postwar decades was the second economic cause of the destruction of the standard Victorian houses of Norwood. In the 1950s, '60s and '70s few people could afford to repair or maintain such establishments, and even fewer foresaw the return of conditions that would bring them back into demand. As a result, private landlords, property developers, and local councils thought only in terms of blanket demolition.

The book includes individual portraits of twenty or so of these lost houses, plus views of several roads that have been almost entirely obliterated. The saddest examples are Hawke Road, where all twenty-nine 1880s houses have been demolished, and the name transferred to a service road that does not even follow the original line; and Tulse Hill, where of 160 houses, some of great beauty, only four or five survive.

The principal published sources of Norwood photographs are Nicholas Reed's *Crystal Palace and the Norwoods*, Jill Dudman's *Brixton and Norwood*, J.B. Wilson's *Story of Norwood*, Alan Warwick's *The Phoenix Suburb*, and my own *Norwood Past*. I have tried not to duplicate any pictures found in those works, and although total success in that respect is unlikely, I will be surprised if more than a handful of the images here have appeared previously in book form.

Acknowledgements

The following have kindly allowed me to copy and reproduce valuable postcards from their collections: John Gent (the cards of South Norwood Baths on p. 18, of Harrington Road on p. 20, and of the eastern entrance to Grangewood on p. 30); Anthony Ashby (the card of Forsyte Crescent on p. 46); and Mrs Marion Crossley (All Saints' School staff on p. 36, from which she also identified the teachers).

Ron Elam of Local Yesterdays (tel. 020 8874 8544) supplied the pictures of the Lansdowne Hall on p. 109 and of Sibton House on p. 113, and has generously allowed them to be reproduced. Copies of these and many other London postcards can be obtained from Mr Elam. I also have to thank: the Croydon Local History Library for the photographs of the front of the Grangewood mansion on p. 28 and of Dover Road on p. 75.

My old friend and collaborator John Seaman has continued his good work of finding Norwood postcards for me. The ones of the Congregational Chapel on p. 96 and of Lansdowne Hill on p. 109 are among his recent discoveries.

As the government of Norwood has always been divided between so many authorities the preparation of my Norwood books has taken me to various libraries. For research facilities and advice on this one I am grateful to the staff at the local history libraries and archive offices of Croydon, Lambeth, Bromley, and Southwark, and at the London Metropolitan Archives.

1

Selhurst Road & South Norwood High Street

The buildings of South Norwood High Street have changed very little since this view from the Stanley clock tower was captured, *c.* 1912. The tall shops in the centre have now been converted into the William Stanley pub, which is some compensation for the recent destruction by fire of the old Stanley works in Belgrave Road.

The Lawns, 201b Selhurst Road (seen here *c.* 1909) took over the name and part of the site of the much larger house that stood at the corner of Park Road from about 1860 to 1907. The new Lawns was occupied in the early 1920s by the civil servant and businessman, Sir Leonard Browett (1884–1959). His departure coincided with the arrival of Crystal Palace FC practically at the bottom of his garden.

This photograph of Selhurst Road, showing the view towards the clock tower from Holy Innocents', was probably taken during the First World War. The distant woman with the white skirt is at the corner of Whitworth Road. The houses on the left are nos 221 and 223, Brunswick Villa and Cleveland (or Cleve) House, which are now lonely Victorian survivors in this part of the road. Brunswick Villa served as the South Norwood Branch Polytechnic from 1892 until 1896, when it moved across the road.

Holy Innocents', Selhurst Road, which was built in 1894–5 as the successor to an iron mission church, is a minor work by a major architect, George Frederick Bodley. His plan included a tower, which has not yet been built, but remains a project for the next William Stanley. The east window, seen here, has stained glass by C.E. Kempe.

The Enmore Park Lawn Tennis Club may well have been founded in Enmore Park, where several of the members lived, but by 1910 its ground was at Selhurst Farm, behind 134 to 152 Selhurst Road. Among the events at the 1910 gymkhana, which were 'keenly contested and provoked much mirth', was the Threading Needle Race, the subject of this postcard. It makes the more familiar egg and spoon variety seem like child's play.

The 12½-acre South Norwood Recreation Ground, which had cost Croydon Corporation a little over £7,000 to acquire and lay out, was opened in 1890. The top picture shows the view from the Cargreen Road entrance. The path branching off to the left led eventually to the bandstand, which stood near Tennison Road. It was even closer to the coal depot and railway yard, which cannot have helped the music. The bandstand, which was yet another of W.F. Stanley's gifts, has now gone, like nearly all those in public parks.

Whitworth Road and Oliver Grove were among the main arteries of the ill-fated Selhurst Park estate, which was started with high hopes, but ended in bankruptcies and a football ground. Whitworth Road (above) was created in the late 1870s by Earle Bird, who lived at Park House in Selhurst Road, now the British Legion club. Its side entrance is on the extreme left of this picture. Oliver Grove (below) was laid out in the early 1860s. The South Norwood Baptist church in Holmesdale Road, which can be seen in the distance, was demolished in 1994, but the site is still lying empty. The congregation now uses the former church hall in Oliver Avenue.

Above: The clock tower junction, where Selhurst Road becomes the High Street, and Oliver Grove and Station Road branch to left and right, has some claim to be the centre of South Norwood – though no doubt residents of Portland Road would disagree. It is seen here during the 1909 Christmas Show week, when the whole shopping centre, including Portland Road, was elaborately decorated and illuminated.

The clock tower was unveiled in 1907 as a tribute to William Stanley, the great benefactor of South Norwood, in the year of his golden wedding anniversary. Behind it is the Alliance, a pub that was built in the mid-1860s, during the rapid creation of the High Street.

This is the view from Station Road towards Oliver Grove, in 1907 or shortly after, to judge from the brightness of the clock tower. Oliver Grove originally had four gate piers to mark its status as the principal entrance to the Selhurst Park estate, but the central pair was moved to its current position at the Selhurst Road entrance to the recreation ground in 1902, an event marked by a local bard:

> That some men were glad – and that some could shed tears,
> Re Oliver Grove – and the loss of its piers,
> Was plainly perceived when, with pick-axe and spade,
> The Council's men came, and the onslaught was made.

The reverse view from Oliver Grove to Station Road, *c.* 1920. In the distance is Norwood Junction station, which was opened in 1859. It was the removal of the station here from Portland Road that turned this into the commercial centre of South Norwood.

This photograph of the High Street was taken from the corner of Grosvenor Road, *c.* 1914, and shows the view towards the South Norwood Hill/Portland Road junction. On the left is the Albion pub, which was built in the mid-1860s. The 'teeth' sign above the exasperated woman (whose tram was presumably late) belonged to the South Norwood Dental Surgery on the first floor of no. 66.

The part of the High Street north of Portland Road, seen here from near the Goat House bridge, *c.* 1900, was older and shabbier than the clock tower end. Some of the cottages on the left in this picture were built in the 1840s and '50s, when this was still considered part either of Selhurst or Penge Road.

2

Portland Road & Environs

Penge Road is seen here from the Goat House bridge in the first year or two of the twentieth century. A small part of the original Goat House pub of 1863 is seen on the right. It was rebuilt in its present form in 1936. The handsome group beyond it was Park Terrace, which was built at the same time as the pub. Four of the houses were destroyed during the Second World War, and the fifth did not survive for much longer.

Portland Road, one of the old tracks across Norwood Common, was retained by the 1800 enclosure commissioners and given the name Woodside Road; but others preferred to call it Norwood Road or Morland Road, and after 1836 the north-western end was generally known as Station Hill. The modern name was gradually adopted after the death, in 1854, of the 4th Duke of Portland. That owner of many houses and yachts had lived from time to time at Norwood Grove, and the district was evidently proud of the connection. Portland Road was South Norwood's main shopping centre until the 1860s, when the growth of the High Street threw its converted cottages into the shade.

This photograph, taken in about 1908 between Farley Road and Crowther Road, shows the view towards the railway bridge. The third building from the right is the Duke of Clarence, a pub founded in the mid-1860s as a beerhouse, and had a long, frustrating struggle for a full licence. In 1870 the court was told that there were 'such frequent applications for spirits that it made the landlord and his wife quite miserable to deny them', but the magistrates were unmoved.

The view of Portland Road from the corner of Clifford Road in the early 1920s. The group of shops behind the 'Cooper's' sign was originally known as Portland Terrace. It looks insignificant now, but was imposing in the 1850s, when surrounded only by scattered cottages, and the name soon spread to the whole road.

The altogether more ornate and ugly shops between Sandown Road and Oakley Road, seen here when new, were known as Portland Parade. The roads and shops were built, *c.* 1900, on what had previously been a great wilderness of brickfields.

Above: The South Norwood Baths in Birchanger Road, seen here in about 1910, were opened in 1881 and replaced by the new baths in Portland Road in the late 1960s. The Birchanger Road Board School (now South Norwood Primary), the building on the left, expanded to fill the space of the demolished baths. The Croydon School Board opened their South Norwood school here in 1875. It had been founded three years earlier in a shop in Station Road.

South Norwood's only large country house was Werndee Hall, Stanger Road, which is seen here in 1907. There was a farm on the site in the eighteenth century, but it was probably rebuilt as a fashionable villa in the 1820s. This was known as Woodside House in the 1830s, China Hall in the 1840s, and Werndee Hall from the 1850s. It was rebuilt again in this grotesque style in 1883. After serving as a factory for many years Werndee Hall was demolished in 1984.

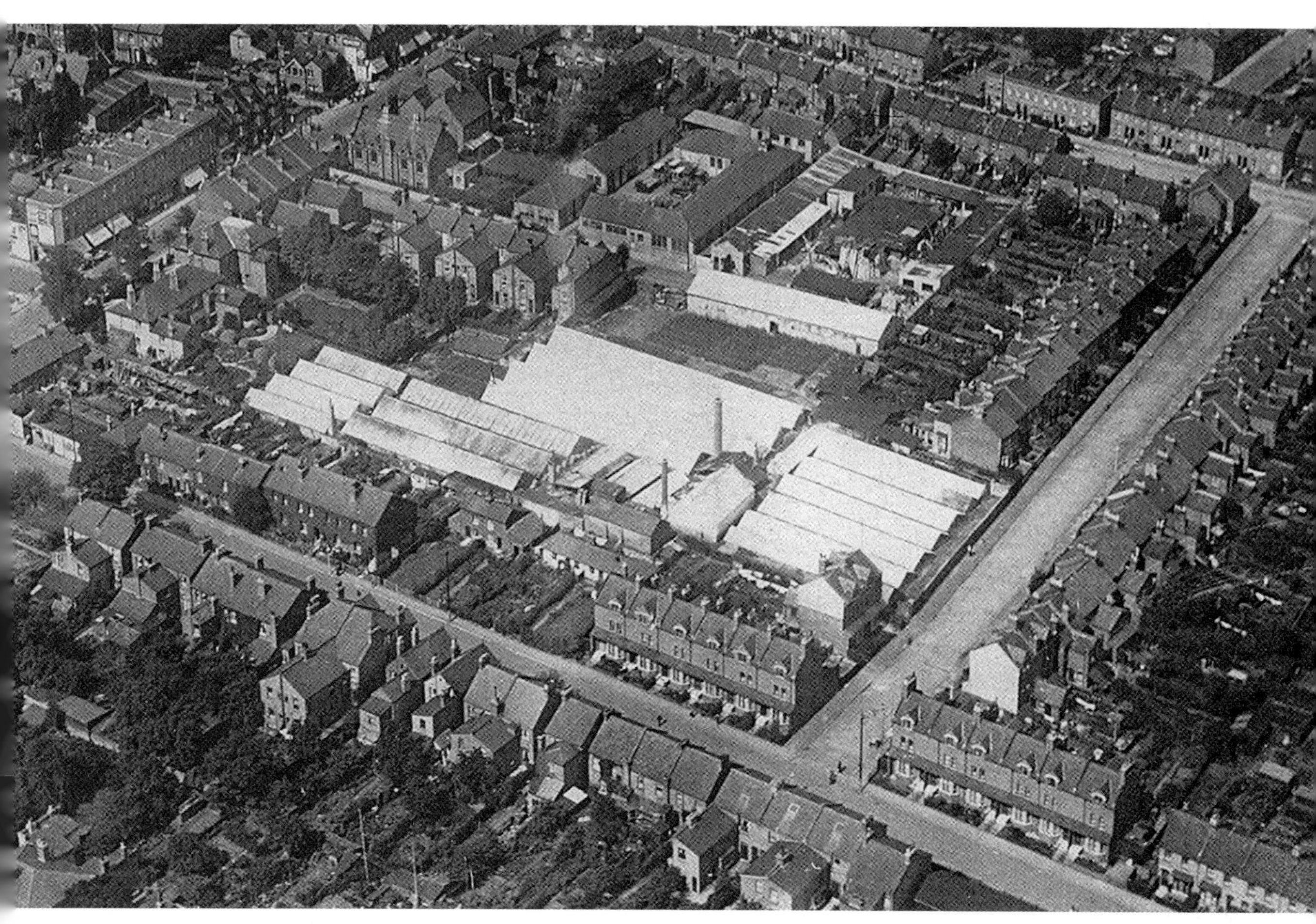

This mid-1920s aerial view shows the block enclosed by Portland Road, at the top left of the picture, Harrington Road at the bottom, Cresswell Road on the right, and Addison Road at the top, with the cul-de-sac of Pembury Road pushing halfway into the interior. The history of this area was intimately connected with two of the houses visible in Portland Road. No. 123 Pembury Villa, the large, detached house with a garden full of trees, just to the left of Pembury Road, was long the home of Horris Parks, whose brickfields formerly occupied most of the land behind. Next door was 125 Morland Villa, half of a pair built in the 1850s. For some sixty years, from the 1880s, it was the home of the Bause family, who were florists.

The white buildings that dominate the centre of the photograph were the glasshouses of the extensive Morland Nursery that the Bauses expanded throughout the first half of the twentieth century. The buildings ranged around a courtyard on the far side of Pembury Road were the workshops of Abner Creasy and Co., who had added the manufacture of motor car bodies to their traditional trade of carriage building. The hall at the corner of Pembury Road and Portland Road is the London City Mission, which was built in 1889. Most of this area was not available for building until the brickfields were closed, but Harrington Road is one of the oldest in South Norwood, and still contains what is probably South Norwood's oldest building. This is 27 King's Acre, the nearest of the four tiny cottages with long front gardens, close to the Morland Nursery glasshouses.

The founding of St Mark's Church at the end of Victoria (now Coventry) Road in 1852 brought Albert Road into being. An Anglican church was a great encouragement to Victorian builders, and a new road was immediately commenced, with housing of a better kind than any available nearby. The church, designed by G.H. Lewis, was largely paid for by the banker John Spofforth Dixon, of Norhyrst in South Norwood Hill. He cannot have been unmindful of the positive effect of this type of development upon the value of his own large estate.

This Edwardian view of Harrington Road was taken from the Portland Road end. The houses on the right are Wilton Villas, Myrtle Cottage, Ada Cottage, Milan Villa, and Ballarat Villa, nos 2 to 12 – Milan Villa was built in the early 1880s, the others in the late 1860s. They all survive.

3

South Norwood Park & Hill

This view up South Norwood Hill from the Whitehorse Lane junction dates from the early 1920s. There was once a horse trough on the traffic island to the left, which has seen many changes. The houses beyond it, north of Whitehorse Lane, were built between 1910 and 1914, and originally called Ross Terrace.

Arundel House, 12 Lancaster Road (which still survives), was built in the late 1860s. This was during the first major expansion of the South Norwood Park estate, which had been commenced a decade earlier. Arundel House was the vicarage of St Mark's from the 1880s to the 1930s, which means that the clergyman standing outside is most likely the Revd John Warner (1860–1933), who was vicar from 1908 until his death.

Most of the original houses of South Norwood Park have been demolished since the war, and the destruction still continues. One of the many lost houses was The Torrs, 5 Warminster Road, which was built in the early 1880s. It is seen here in about 1906, when occupied by Robert Davidson.

Norwood Lake, which estate agents have taken to referring to in the plural, as though it were in Cumberland, is the surviving reservoir of the Croydon Canal. This and its long lost partner at Sydenham were used to collect water from feeder streams to top up the canal as necessary. Since 1836, and more formally since 1881, it has been put to recreational uses: sailing, swimming, skating, fishing, and the racing of model boats. The footpath around the lake (seen here *c.* 1920) became a favourite shady promenade for the members of the Norwood Club, who enjoyed it in lofty solitude until the 1930s.

Woodvale Avenue was probably created shortly after 1806, when the piece of common land of which it formed the southern edge was sold and enclosed. Oddly enough, the newly fenced field to the north was not built upon for 120 years. On the south side two villas of the 1830s, Woodvale Lodge and Woodvale House, enjoyed nearly a century of exclusive use of the road. This 1920s scene, captured from near the point where Norhyrst Avenue now branches off, and looking east towards Lancaster Road, would not have appeared much different at any time between 1840 and 1925. Development of the north-west side (the left in the picture) began from the South Norwood Hill end in 1926, and was complete by 1929. Most of the houses on the south side were built, partly on the site of Woodvale House, in the early 1930s. Woodvale Lodge, at the corner of South Norwood Hill, became the Woodvale Social Club, and survived until 1959.

The most important memorials to William Stanley are the Stanley Halls and Technical School in South Norwood Hill. He designed them himself, and built them in stages between 1902 and 1909, the committee rooms and secretary's house being incomplete when Stanley died in that year. The top picture shows the first part, the large hall, as it looked when opened in 1903. At that stage 12 and 14 South Norwood Hill, a pair of houses built in 1875–6, and uninspiringly called The Villas, were still standing next door. A part of no. 14 can be seen on the right. The photograph below, taken *c.* 1912, shows the committee rooms on the site of The Villas, and beyond them the full range of buildings. The sign at the corner of Suffolk Road (on the left) is a reminder that the South Norwood fire station was at 5 to 9 South Norwood Hill, now shops, until the early 1930s.

The South Norwood Wesleyan Church in South Norwood Hill was built in 1874, as the successor to a chapel in Portland Road. The architect was Alexander Lander. This photograph was taken in the early 1900s from William Stanley's drive, which is now Cumberlow Avenue. The church was demolished in 1977, but the congregation continues to meet in the hall in Suffolk Road.

Below: St Cuthbert's, 33 Ross Road, was built in 1880 for a retired merchant's clerk who must have enjoyed a remarkable pension scheme. It was a huge house with a garden stretching down to Whitehorse Lane, and as the fortunes of Norwood declined such an expensive luxury inevitably became an institution – a Salvation Army girls' home – in 1923. These front and garden views were taken in about 1930. St Cuthbert's was demolished in the 1980s, when Cuthbert Gardens was built on the

One of the many ornate Victorian houses in South Norwood Hill, of which so few remain, was Nettlestead, no. 252, which was later known as Tordarrach. It was built in approximately 1890, and demolished in the 1960s to make room for part of Dorrington Court. The site was opposite Grange Gardens. This photograph was probably taken just before the First World War, when John Mitchell lived at Nettlestead.

The finest of all South Norwood Hill houses is Spurgeon's College, the Baptist theological seminary, which is seen here in the 1920s; but it turns its back on the world, appearing from the road like an ugly hospital behind a garage. This is the pleasant surprise that awaits those who venture up the drive. The college authorities have sold much land since the war, but the fine lawn seen in the foreground is happily intact. The house was built in 1889 for the tea merchant Thomas McMeekin, to the designs of H.A. Rawlins. McMeekin called his house Falkland Park, and both that name and the present one have caused confusion. A popular canard is that this was once the residence of Viscount Falkland, whose house stood much closer to Grange Hill. It is now sometimes said that Spurgeon's College belonged to C.H. Spurgeon, whereas the name was merely a tribute to the great Baptist who had lived nearby, at Westwood in Beulah Hill.

4

Grangewood

This fine old oak used to provide a pleasantly shady resting place at the top of the sharp hill from the southern, or Thornton Heath, gate of Grangewood. The tree still stands, minus the two lowest branches, but the welcome seats have gone. The view is from the north, with the path to the gate on the right.

Grangewood House was designed by an architect named Brown, and built in 1861 for the iron merchant and inventor Charles Hood (1805–89). The estate was auctioned after his death and only a determined campaign led by Thomas McMeekin of Falkland Park (see p. 26) prevented its becoming a fever hospital. The council opened it as a park in 1901 and the mansion was used as a museum run, eccentrically enough, by the Roads Committee. The park keeper seen on the veranda in the Edwardian view of the garden front is perhaps J. Jeffreys. The photograph of the main entrance (below) was taken in the mid-1950s, shortly before the house was demolished.

There was no southern entrance to Charles Hood's estate, nor any plantation in the point of the triangle between Grange Road and Ross Road, so the council had to lay out the flower beds and create the path and gates. The attractive Thornton Heath Lodge was built in 1902. It survives in good condition, but the open porch has been enclosed to form a lobby.

The Grangewood Lodge at the northern end of the park was built at the same time as the mansion, and was originally occupied by the gate keeper. This path was the carriage drive to Charles Hood's front door. The gate house is now called Wharnecliffe Lodge.

The eastern gate of Grangewood seen from Canham Road, *c.* 1910. The Ross Road Cottage, which stood at the top of the steps until the 1980s, was also contemporary with the mansion, and built for Hood's gardener. A glimpse of it can be seen on p. 32. One hopes the gardener was not a big man, as the rooms of the cottage were extraordinarily small.

One of the many attractions of the old Grangewood (most of them destroyed in the 1950s and '60s) was the piece of water known bombastically as the lake. It lay towards the southern end of the park, close to Grange Road. The beauty of the lake owed most to the encircling trees, but art assisted with a huge rockery along the eastern side and the two bridges seen in these Edwardian photographs. The rustic bridge crossed the lake near its southern end. The plainer bridge took the path across the northern feeder stream.

The original bowling green at Grangewood was laid out between 1909 and 1911, and the pretty pavilion was built in 1912, shortly before these photographs were taken. (A green had been suggested in 1903, but the estimate of £149 frightened the council.) The bottom picture, from the pavilion, looks across to the higher ground that was used as a kitchen garden in Hood's day. The gardener's cottage can be seen beyond it. It was on the site of the kitchen garden that the present bowling green was created in 1934–5. The old green was then given over to the ladies, but they abandoned it in the 1970s, and after a spell as a children's play area it is now disused.

The bandstand, one of the first attractions added to the park, was the gift of Lady Edridge, the Mayoress, in 1903. It stood almost in the centre of Grangewood, just to the west of the old bowling green. The bandstand was still occasionally used for concerts in the 1950s, but soon afterwards fell a victim to economies, vandalism and changing tastes in music.

This is the other end of Charles Hood's carriage drive (see p. 30), as it appeared from the front of the mansion – or today, alas, from the sunken garden. Its municipal name was the broad walk. The circular flower bed survives, as does the tall pine on the left.

These steps, which led from the mansion towards the Ross Road Cottage and the kitchen garden, would have been a useful short cut in Hood's days at Grangewood, but the evidence of maps suggests that they were constructed by the council during the laying out of the park. The scene is little changed, except that a tall tree has grown to the left of the steps in the eighty years or so since the photograph was taken.

5

Beulah Hill

Spa Close and the shops in South Norwood Hill on either side were built in 1933 on the site of the Old Spa House, one of Norwood's early mansions. This photograph was taken when the road was very new.

The staff of All Saints' School, *c.* 1925. They were, back row, left to right: Mr Agar, Miss Jeffard, Mr Cartwright (headmaster and church organist), Miss Beale, Mr Williams, Miss Jarvis. Front row: Miss Bailey (teacher for class 1 – 'a very kind lady') and Miss Martin. The old school buildings in the background were demolished in 1964, the headmaster's house in 1972.

The view west along Beulah Hill from the corner of Upper Beulah Hill, *c.* 1910. The large houses on the right were Courtlands and Thornton, nos 6 and 8. They were both built in 1868 and demolished in 1938. In the distance can be seen the post office and other shops towards Harold Road that were pulled down in the 1960s.

The philanthropic carpet manufacturer Sir William Purdie Treloar (1843–1923), who served as Lord Mayor of London in 1907–8, was an Upper Norwood resident for nearly half his life. He occupied 281 Church Road (which perhaps deserves a plaque) from about 1889 to 1896, and Grangemount, 13 Beulah Hill (now demolished), until his death.

Another of the ornate houses that occupied the road frontage of the Beulah Spa grounds was Westview, 19 Beulah Hill, which was built in about 1860. The garden front is seen here early in the twentieth century, when a Mrs Ormiston was the tenant. Like the great majority of these houses Westview fell into disrepair after the war, and was demolished when the original lease expired.

A 1920s view of Beulah Hill, taken from outside the Beulah Spa Hotel, showing the entrances to Harold Road on the left and Spa Hill on the right. The large building behind the lamppost is Yarrow House, 35 Beulah Hill, the only survivor of the villas built in the spa grounds during the 1850s and '60s, but this year ruined by a greedy garden extension. To the right is the estate lodge, dated '1864'.

This 1920s photograph of the Beulah Spa Hotel is almost the reverse of the one above. The hotel was built in 1831 to accommodate visitors to the mineral spring, but was in serious decline by 1920. The house beyond it, with the 'Turkish Baths' sign on the wall, was Ashtree, no. 45. It had been built early in the nineteenth century as one of a pair, but the other half, Spa Cottage, was incorporated with the hotel, and demolished in the 1890s.

These photographs of the rear of the Beulah Spa, and of the hotel garden, were taken in the late 1920s or early '30s, when Arthur Monk was the proprietor. The building on the left of the top picture was the ballroom that replaced Spa Cottage in the 1890s. The hotel had struggled to justify its size ever since the closure of the spa pleasure grounds in 1856, and Arthur Monk was to be its last master. It was demolished in 1937 and the present pub was built on a part of the site soon afterwards.

The Upper Norwood Recreation Ground was opened in 1890. Today it fills the space between Eversley, Chevening, Hermitage, and Harold Roads, but originally it did not extend to the last two. This 1920s view from near Eversley Road shows the bandstand (added in 1895, but now of course removed) and St Margaret's in Chevening Road, a mission church of All Saints' built in 1903.

Queen's Road, which has been known as Queen Mary Road since December 1938, began in the 1860s as a cul-de-sac off Crown Hill (or Dale as it is now called) and took until 1900 to reach Beulah Hill. This photograph was taken from the southern end soon afterwards, and shows the other All Saints' mission hall, which was established in the early 1900s and lasted until the mid-1960s. The flats known as Tudor House are now on the site.

This splendid collection of schoolboys, teachers, priests, and nuns (not to mention the dog) was assembled in the garden of Norbury Hill House, probably in 1915 or 1916. It stood on the north side of Norbury Hill, about 100 yards south-west of the Conquering Hero pond. Its origin was an eighteenth-century cottage, built as an encroachment on the common, which grew into a substantial villa after the enclosure of 1800. Norbury Hill House was evidently rebuilt in the middle of the nineteenth century, probably for the hat manufacturer Henry Ellwood, who was the owner from the 1840s to the 1860s. It was described as 'one of the most perfect properties near London' when auctioned in 1898, but demand for such lavish houses in Norwood was falling, and it lay empty for some years until taken over by St Joseph's College (see p. 43) in 1905. Many of the teaching brothers were refugees from France, and they usually lived in the house, but during the First World War it served as a Belgian school and a military hospital. The photograph probably shows the staff and pupils of St Mary's College, which is mentioned in the history of St Joseph's: 'The "White House" `in Norbury was called into use again when a group of Belgian refugees, consisting of pupils and Brothers from one of the schools of the invaded country, sought shelter there.' Between the wars the sloping grounds were gradually terraced to adapt them for use as playing fields. The mansion was demolished at about the time of the Second World War, but probably not as a result of bomb damage.

Sir August Manns (1825–1907), the great conductor of the Crystal Palace orchestra through all its years of glory from 1855 until 1900, lived in at least four Norwood houses. The earliest known, 135 Knight's Hill, perhaps deserves a commemorative plaque, as the only survivor. Manns was later at 4 Dulwich Wood Park, 4 Harold Road, and during the last year of his life (when this photograph was taken) at White Lodge, Biggin Hill.

The Croydon enclosure commissioners made special provision that a pond opposite the Rose and Crown pub should 'remain open for the use of the public as heretofore'. That pond vanished long ago, but this one beside the Conquering Hero, dismissed in 1800 as 'a large pond or gravel pit' is still a valued ornament of Beulah Hill. The board in the background advertises land for sale on the site of Springfield, a house demolished in 1906.

St Joseph's College, one of London's leading Catholic secondary schools, was opened at Clapham in 1855, and had spells at Tooting and Denmark Hill before moving to Norwood in 1903/4. The new home was Grecian Villa, which is seen on the left in this 1920s photograph. It was a two-storey house of eighteenth-century origin, but perhaps rebuilt in 1839. The attic storey was added in 1903 to provide dormitories. The chapel, on the right, was built in 1913 to the designs of Bernard McAdam, who had been educated at the original school in Tooting.

This area to the north of the chapel is still a playing field as it was *c.* 1904, but lawn tennis is no longer the favoured game. Beyond Beulah Hill on the right is the field on which Grecian Crescent was soon to be laid out. The three houses in the background were built in 1884. The nearer two still stand, and are occupied by college staff. The first one, Glencar, was the principal's house from the 1920s.

Norwood's finest surviving house, and one of its great estates since 1760, is Norwood Grove, which was saved from the destruction that has overtaken nearly all the other estates when it became a park in 1926. The plaque in this late 1920s photograph records the part played in the preservation campaign by Stenton Covington (1856–1935), a prominent member of the National Trust who lived in Gibson's Hill. The lodge seen in the picture below guarded the gate leading from the Norwood Grove grounds to those of The Rookery. It is now known as 11 Copgate Lane.

6

Church Road

Church Road is seen here from the corner of Fox Hill, with the garden of Norbury Lodge on the left, *c.* 1914. On the right are the gate of Westow Villa (now Rosetta Court), the matching 1860s pair of Beaufort House and Argyle House (now both hotels), and the massive flank of the Queen's Hotel.

All Saints', the parish church of Upper Norwood, was designed by James Savage and built between 1827 and 1829. The tower and spire were added in 1841. Sadly little remains of the gothic gates that still adorned the churchyard when this photograph was taken, *c.* 1912.

Below: Hazelwood, an early 1860s house of such luxury that it was once rumoured the Prince of Wales (Edward VII) intended to buy it, lay derelict in the 1920s after rough usage from soldiers during and after the war. In 1934 Forsyte Crescent, seen here when just completed, was built on the site. The lodge of Hazlewood survived for a time as 295 Church Road, and can be glimpsed below the trees on the far left. In the distance is part of Dilston House, no. 291, which was built in about 1868, and destroyed by bombing during the Second World War.

Sylvan Hill (seen here from Church Road, *c.* 1912) was a mere farm track until the development of Auckland Road in the 1870s. On the left was the 2-acre garden of All Saints' vicarage, and on the right the larger grounds of Oakhurst, which extended to Auckland Road.

On the left of this 1920s view is Beulah Villa, 124 Church Road, the Swiss style of which comes into its own in these conditions. The house was built in 1835–6. Beyond it the great bulk of the Queen's Hotel is almost obscured by mist and trees.

The Queen's Hotel was the largest and most successful of several founded during the first rush of Crystal Palace enthusiasm to cater for the hordes of visitors. It was built in 1853–4, at the same time as the Palace. During its first fifty years it attracted numerous fashionable and even illustrious guests, including the Emperor Frederick of Germany, Florence Nightingale, John Bright, Angela Burdett-Coutts, and Émile Zola, whose stay in 1898–9 is commemorated by a blue plaque. The ideas of the hotel's architect, Francis Pouget, can still be appreciated in these pre-1914 photographs, but in recent decades fire, demolitions, and extensions have obscured them. To emphasise the changes to the building and clientele in characteristic modern fashion, the owners have recently given it a new name, the Quality Hotel.

Walmer, 108 Church Road, formerly known as Westow House or Gladswood, was built in the early 1820s and originally used as Edward Pizey's boarding school for boys. The Royal Normal College for the Blind (see p. 66) bought it as additional accommodation in 1896, and after the college closed it was used by Croydon Council for homeless families. The house was demolished in 1969 and the site taken to extend Westow Park. The *c.* 1905 view above shows the garden front. In the slightly later picture below the gates of Walmer can be seen on the left. They have been retained as a decorative feature in the park wall. Hope Cottage at the corner of Fox Hill (on the right) has also survived.

In a triumph of piety over commerce, the Upper Norwood war memorial, which was unveiled in 1922, took the place of the White Hart signpost on the island at the junction of Church Road and Westow Street, as seen here soon after. This was itself a second choice site. The favoured location, at the Vicar's Oak junction, was vetoed by the traffic authorities. By 1956 traffic had got entirely the upper hand of piety, and the memorial was moved to its present, far less prominent, position in front of the supermarket in Westow Street.

Below: This view from the Upper Norwood Congregational Church towards the south tower of the Crystal Palace dates from *c.* 1904. The hoardings, the nearest one advertising sites for villas, are on the former frontage of Cintra, the large 1830s house that was demolished just after 1900. The gate on the right belonged to Spring Grove House, a contemporary of Cintra that survived until 1984. Nightingale Court has taken its place.

7

Auckland Road to Anerley Hill

Anerley Hill from the corner of Crystal Palace Station Road, with the Paxton Arms Hotel on the left. The date is apparently 1902, as one of the placards outside the post office refers to the Education Bill. David Porter, who ran the post office, combined it, unusually, with a bakery.

This view up Belvedere Road from Maberley Road was probably captured on the same day as the photograph on p. 53. The houses on the right, up to Maberley Crescent, were built in 1875 as Belvedere Villas. They are now numbered 111 to 101.

Belvedere College, 89 Belvedere Road, *c.* 1905. It was built in the early 1860s, and known at first as The Ferns. In the 1870s, and perhaps earlier, its tenants held the lease of the Belvedere Green opposite. The Ferns was used as a boarding school from 1880, for boys for a year or two and then for girls until the First World War. The last schoolmistress was Miss Frances Eleanor Smith, whose notice-board appears in this picture.

The delightful Belvedere Road is unusually well preserved for Norwood, but even here a number of the Victorian houses have been demolished. Part of one can be seen on the extreme left of this photograph. Aspen House, no. 66, was built in 1854 for William Wright Stanger, JP, who presumably gave his name to the road in South Norwood. He might more obviously have given it to Palace Grove, which he built at the end of his garden, also in 1854; but instead he tried, with little success, to call it Greenland Terrace. Even with Palace Grove subtracted, the size of its garden proved the undoing of Aspen House: Sutton Court was built over it in the mid-1960s, and the house was demolished to provide access. This view up Belvedere Road from the green probably dates from the 1920s. There is certainly no trace of the Belvedere College notice-board (see p. 52) in the garden of no. 89 on the right, which suggests that it was no longer a school. The houses seen on that side are nos 87 and 85, Ingoldsby and Ramsdale, a pair built in about 1884.

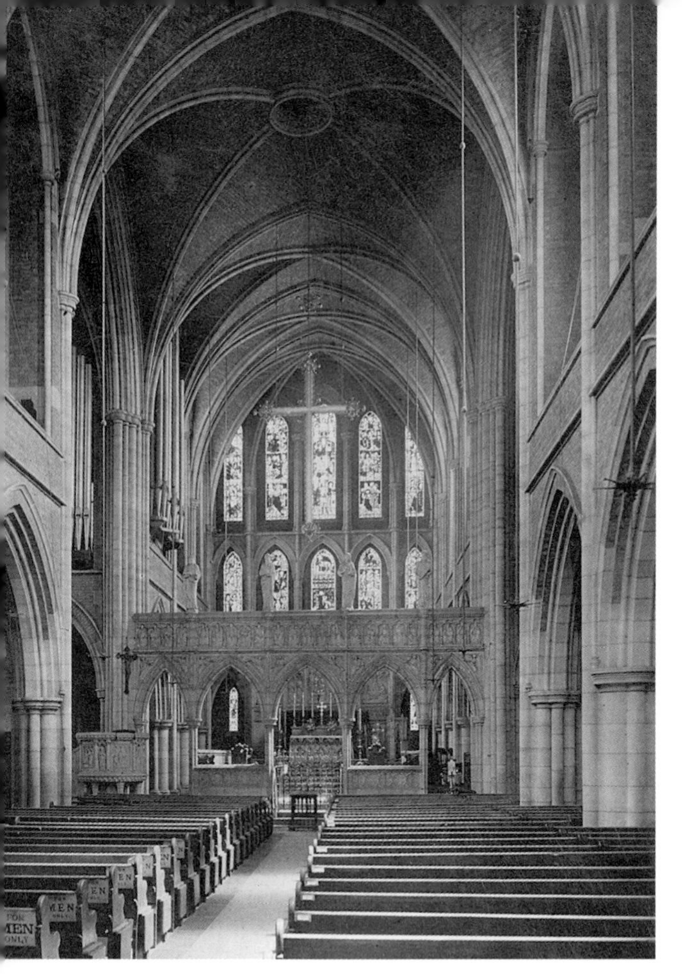

St John's, Auckland Road, designed by John Loughborough Pearson and built between 1881 and 1887, is Norwood's most memorable church. It was badly damaged during the war, but has been well restored.

Below: From 1880 until 1936 the vicars of St John's lived at 107 Auckland Road, although it did not officially become the vicarage until 1909. The vicar seen in the garden here is Henry Sutherland Dashwood Gill, who was more noted as a golfer than a theologian. He once went twice round the adjacent 9 hole Norwood course in 59. In this 1920s photograph the house on the right is no. 80 (Monkswood), which, like the vicarage, has now been demolished.

One of the largest surviving houses in Auckland Road is Hillside, no. 151, built in 1888. When this view was taken, probably in the 1920s, it could still be seen as a whole, but the growth of the trees has since made it practically impossible to photograph.

Belvedere Green, at the meeting point of Auckland Road, Fox Hill, and Belvedere Road, is still one of the chief attractions of this well-preserved area, though it looks worn and untidy when compared with this glimpse from before the First World War, when it was still enclosed. The green long pre-dates Auckland Road, and appears to have been created as part of the Belvedere Road/Hamlet Road development of the 1850s.

Hamlet Road, which is presumably named after the Hamlet of Penge rather than the Prince of Denmark, had its origin in a bridle path through Anerley Wood. Building began in about 1850 and accelerated after the coming of the Crystal Palace. This view towards Anerley Road, dating from 1916 or earlier, shows Salisbury House (built in about 1860) on the left and St Paul's Church in the centre. The church was built in 1866, demolished in 1973/4, and replaced in 1978.

A fragment of wood survived above Hamlet Road for twenty-five years, and was the lurking place of the Anerley Grove flasher in 1866. It was through this wood that Waldegrave Road was laid out in the mid-1870s. Development was slow. The Swedenborgian church, seen in this Edwardian postcard, was not built until 1883. Its material makes it interesting to architectural historians: the design was by W.J.E. Henley, manager of the Concrete Building Company. The church was closed in 1987, and converted into flats.

The North Surrey District School in Anerley Road was the junior branch of the workhouse for the contributing parishes. It was opened in 1850, and survived until the abolition of workhouses in 1930. It became the LCC's Anerley District School, and later the Orchard Lodge old people's home, and was demolished in the 1970s. The school regime must have been liberalised by the 1920s, when this reasonably cheerful group of inmates was clearly performing *The Pirates of Penzance*.

Crystal Palace station is today a pitiful wreck of a great monument of railway architecture. Decay had begun even when this photograph was taken in about 1913, as the roof that originally linked the two massive walls was removed some seven years before because of fears about its safety. What is seen here was the first part of the station. It was the terminus for trains from London Bridge via Sydenham from 1854 until 1856, when the tracks were extended to Gipsy Hill and points west. The line from Norwood Junction was added in 1857.

Two views of Anerley Hill from the corner of Hadlow Place, both *c.* 1918. In the bottom picture the entrance to Waldegrave Road is on the left. The turning below the south tower of the Crystal Palace in both views is Anerley Vale. The white-faced building at its corner was the Rising Sun, no. 72, a pub founded in the mid-nineteenth century by William Nowell, a hatter who took up beer-selling as a sideline. It was a notoriously noisy house in the 1860s, when violent disputes were provoked by such questions as what Mrs Scott, the landlord's wife, wore beneath her crinoline. The Rising Sun was badly damaged in the Blitz, and demolished in the early 1950s.

The kitchens of the Royal Crystal Palace Hotel in the 1920s. The hotel was built in 1853 at the corner of Anerley Hill and Church Road, and largely destroyed by bombing during the Second World War. The condition of the part that survives in Church Road is a disgrace even to Bromley Council.

The Crystal Palace, *c.* 1920. In the left foreground are Westow Hill and St Aubuyn's Road. At bottom right can be seen the houses on the north side of Milestone Road, built on the site of Cintra from *c.* 1907. The south side remained undeveloped for twenty years more. In Anerley Hill, above Milestone Road, note not only the surviving Harefield House (no. 14) but its lost companion The Hermitage. They are the second and third buildings to the right of the water tower. For the points of interest in the Crystal Palace Park see another aerial view on p. 65.

The Crystal Palace School of Practical Engineering was very much the family business of the Wilsons, who occupied the post of Principal for all but the last four years of its existence. The Crystal Palace Company opened the school in 1872, at the urging of Joseph William Wilson (1829–98), who ran it until his death. He was succeeded by his son and namesake, who is the dominating figure fifth from the left in the front row of this 1906 group. The staff and students are posed not far from the premises of the school, in the south tower and what is now the Crystal Palace Museum in Anerley Hill. They were not to have their home here for much longer. Wars had a sinister influence on the history of the school. The takeover of the Crystal Palace by the Royal Navy in 1914 meant that the second J.W. Wilson (1851–1930) had to find alternative accommodation across the road at the former Star Hotel, now 18 Anerley Hill. In 1930 Maurice Wilson (1862–1936), another son of the founder, moved the school to its last address at Harefield House, 14 Anerley Hill. It was there that the story ended in 1940, when the last Principal, Frederick C.P. Lawrence, who had taken over on the death of Maurice Wilson, found that all the nation's young engineers were receiving urgent practical training at the expense of the state.

8

Parade & Triangle

The Grosvenor Building of the Royal Normal College for the Blind (see p. 66) was named in honour of the 1st Duke of Westminster, a generous supporter of the charity. It was opened in 1878 and demolished in the 1960s, with most of the other College buildings. The Secret Garden nursery now occupies the site. This 1920s photograph was taken from Bedwardine Road.

This view towards Anerley Hill from Westow Hill is dominated, like so many others, by the south tower of the Crystal Palace. On the right is a less common glimpse of the Royal Crystal Palace Hotel (see p. 59), at the corner of Church Road. The top of Anerley Hill was the terminus for Croydon trams from 1905, when this photograph was taken.

The founders of the White Swan in Westow Hill were lucky enough to acquire what was soon to be a prime site before the Crystal Palace was thought of. After 1854 the pub quckly grew from a humble beershop to the large inn shown in this 1883 photograph. Soon afterwards it was rebuilt on three floors. Its decline has also followed the Crystal Palace. The third storey was removed in the 1960s, and the garishly painted fragment is now called Bluebottle.

Two photographs of Crystal Palace Parade, both apparently taken from the roof of the Cambridge Hotel. The letting of this vantage point must have been a useful supplement to the landlord's income. The top picture was probably taken during the First World War, the other in the early 1930s. The Parade has rarely been without an array of buses at any date. The bottom picture shows, on the left, the roof of the Crystal Palace High Level station. The curving building at the corner of Farquhar Road, next to the station, was a coal merchant's office.

An unusual view of the High Level station, framed in the entrance of the College Road tunnel. The photograph was taken in 1957, near the midpoint of dereliction between the closing of the line in 1954 and the demolition of the station in 1961. Spinney Gardens was built on the site of the tracks and platforms in the early 1980s.

The central transept entrance of the Crystal Palace in 1928, with a fine collection of 'Notices of Entertainments' posted outside. Attractions included Saturday dances, Corinthian Football Club matches, and 'high-class entertainment' in the Picture House, a cinema within the Palace that was open from 1925 until 1930. The high-class films on offer during this week included *His Dog* and *Glad Eye*.

This aerial view of the Crystal Palace was taken in 1920 or earlier, by one of the companies set up after the war to exploit the talents of demobilised pilots. It shows the park still cluttered with the three-quarter-scale replicas of the parliament buildings of Australia, Canada, etc., etc., that were built for the Festival of Empire in 1911. Towards the top left of the picture can be seen the 'flying machine' constructed by Sir Hiram Maxim (see p. 112) in 1904. The lake at bottom left took the place of the north transept of the Palace, which was destroyed by fire in 1866. It became an elaborate feature during the Festival of Empire, with replica buildings on the islands and a water splash fed by the tanks on stilts. The right hand side of the photograph features the High Level station, with the tracks extending to the tunnel under College Road (see p. 64). On the extreme right is the curve of Farquhar Road, with its large Victorian houses still intact.

The Royal Normal College and Academy of Music for the Blind was the creation of two remarkable men, Thomas Armitage and Francis Campbell, both themselves blind. It was founded in 1872 in Anerley Hill, but in the next year began moving to The Mount in Westow Street (left), a house built in 1816–17. Numerous annexes were built or acquired over the next twenty years (see, for example, pp. 49 and 61), but the roof seen rising above The Mount here was not part of the College property. It was the immensely tall 68 Westow Street, originally part of a draper's shop, then for years a temperence billiards hall, and finally Barker's piano shop. The photograph below shows a patriotic wartime entertainment at the College in 1916, in which the girls wore the costumes of all the allied nations. Note the kimono dancing with the sari.

In the Crystal Palace triangle Westow Street had to cede the first place to Westow Hill, which was the equal of most West End shopping centres. In Westow Street the quality of the buildings and businesses was less consistently good. The photograph above was taken outside the Royal Normal College, the wall of which appears on the left. The supermarket now occupies this area, but most of the shops on the right survive. The picture below was taken near the corner of Central Hill. The clock outside Gaydon & Sons, the watchmakers of nos 16 to 20, has now crossed the road to the Foresters' Hall, which can be seen in the middle distance. It was built in 1877 as the Welcome Coffee Tavern.

The cottage behind 41 Westow Street is one of the oldest buildings surviving in the Triangle. From 1819 or earlier until the 1850s it was occupied by John Cresswell, a 'stuff melter', which probably meant that he boiled down meat scraps for the fat. The shopfront was most likely added in the early 1870s when a long-running greengrocery business was founded at nos 41 and 43. It was run by James Chittell from 1875 until 1911. Percy Turley then took over no. 41 only – this photograph was perhaps taken to mark the change of ownership – and he and his family remained until the Second World War. The shop is now occupied by a barber. On the left of the picture can be seen some of the cottages on the north side of Victory Place that were demolished in 1938. It is hard to say which victory this alley celebrated. It probably existed from the time of Waterloo, but there was little development until the 1850s, and I have not seen the name recorded before 1876.

Opposite: The Wesleyan Church spire appears in this 1904 photograph, but the interest is in the three shops. On the left is no. 33, which was occupied by Jules Johann Weiss, a confectioner. Parke's Drug Store was no. 35, and no. 37 was the shop of the tea and wine merchant Charles Frederick Buxton, who is standing proudly in the doorway. He sent the picture to a girlfriend who lived in Becondale Road.

The Upper Norwood Wesleyans began to meet at a chapel in Gipsy Hill in the early 1860s. It survives as the printing works now numbered 16. In 1874 they moved to the much grander Westow Street Church, designed by Charles Bell, that is shown in this postcard of *c.* 1905. It was demolished in 1963 so that a temple of Mammon, or supermarket, could take its place, with a new church hidden behind.

One of the many smart shops in Westow Hill belonged to R.S. and A.P. Cufflin, watchmakers and jewellers, whose showroom is seen here in the 1920s. They claimed to have been established in 1837, but first appeared at no. 67, as Stephens and Cufflin, in 1884.

This view of Westow Hill just before the First World War features, as usual, the south water tower of the Crystal Palace. It was taken from Woodland Street. In the immediate foreground was the Crystal Palace Floral Hall, as A.E. Blundell called his little, single-storey flower shop at no. 57. The canopy beyond what is now Barclays Bank belonged to the Electra Picture Palace at no. 63. On the right, at the far corner of St Aubyn's Road, was a large branch of W.H. Smith, 'the Strand Bookshop', at no. 70.

9

Central Hill, Crown Hill & Environs

An Edwardian view of the part of the Convent of the Faithful Virgin (see p. 76) that faces Central Hill. On the right is the St Joseph's Wing, built in 1862 to house the Catholic infant paupers snatched from the North Surrey District School (see p. 57). Beyond it are the Bishop Grant Memorial Hall and, at right angles, the chapel.

Two views of the eastern end of Central Hill, looking towards Westow Hill just before the First World War (above), and from the crossroads in the mid-1920s. The trees mask the large houses on the Lambeth side of Central Hill. With their north-facing gardens they were never so popular as the ones on the Croydon side. Many were bought by Lambeth Council between the wars for conversion into flats, and in the 1960s they were all swept away to make room for the new estates. The shops behind the traffic policeman have been built over the front gardens of cottages that are among the oldest buildings in Central Hill.

Central Hill, *c*. 1920. The 1850s pair in the distance (nos 23 and 25) was Merton Villas. Central Hill Baptist church was built in 1852 and demolished in 1955 or soon after. The only surviving house in the picture is Gatestone, no. 29, which stands on the near corner of Gatestone Road, to which it gave its name. It was built in the mid-1870s for Sir Sidney Smith Saunders, who was British consul in Albania and the Ionian Isles. On the right is Scotland House, which was built in about 1820, and originally had extensive grounds. It was wrecked during the Second World War. One of its lodges was removed to make room for Gatestone Road.

In this 1920s view eastwards from Essex Grove the right or Croydon side of Central Hill looks much as it does today, but everything on the Lambeth side has been demolished. The nearest house on the left was Wyattville, no. 66.

Gatestone Road was a development of the late 1870s across the former garden of Scotland House (see p. 73). The oldest house, no. 4, is dated '1878'. This *c.* 1914 photograph was taken from Bedwardine Road, and shows in the distance 29 Central Hill, the house after which the road was named.

The Ecclesiastical Commissioners, the owners of much of the land between Central Hill and Beulah Hill, projected Harold Road in the 1870s, but building did not begin until the early 1880s. The oldest examples in this road of remarkable houses are nos 34 to 48. Dell House (no. 52), Highcroft (no. 54), etc., seen here from the Bedwardine Road corner just before the First World War, date from the late 1880s and early '90s.

Norwood New Town, the curious working-class enclave on the south side of Central Hill, in the heart of middle-class Upper Norwood, was built in the 1850s and entirely demolished by Croydon Council in the 1960s. This was the north side of Dover Road in 1960, with Oxford Road in the distance. The thirteen houses and two shops were known as Albert Terrace. The shop at the corner of Naseby Road (29 Dover Road, formerly 15 Albert Terrace) can be traced back to the 1850s. For the first sixty years it was used by a succession of bakers: John King, Richard Wheatley, John Stevens, Samuel Collier, Charles Townsend, and Mrs Susan Townsend. It was a sweet shop during the First World War, a drapery in the early 1920s, and then a newsagent's and confectioner's again until its demolition. The last proprietors, the Fosters, 'sold a variety of sweets: Jamboree bags at 2*d*, loose lemonade powder and liquorice wood sticks. Mrs Foster also made her own ice lollies: small 1*d*, large 2*d*, and large trays of toffee which had to be broken up with a small hammer'.

The Convent of the Faithful Virgin in Central Hill (originally Notre Dame des Orphelines) was founded in 1848 by nuns from Normandy. The property they acquired was the Park Hotel, formerly Park House, and famous in the eighteenth century as the home of the adventuress Mary Nesbit. The extensive grounds gave ample scope for expansion. The first new building was added in 1857, and many others followed over the next seventy years. The chapel (see p. 71) was built in 1881 to the designs of Edward Goldie. The Fidelis school (of which the art room, or art corridor, is shown below in about 1920) was established for 'young ladies of the higher classes', to raise income for the convent's work with orphans.

The roads to the north of Central Hill have suffered severely since 1945, and the scenes shown in these *c.* 1912 views have been obliterated. Victoria Road, a development of the 1860s, became Victoria Crescent in 1936. Between 1977 and 1979 the middle section was replaced by a council estate, and the now detached northern end was re-named Mountbatten Close. In the photograph above, looking towards Gipsy Hill station, only the most distant building survives. Hawke Road (below), which was built from 1881 and originally called Globe Road, has fared even worse. Every Victorian house that survived the war was swept away in the 1960s to accommodate the Central Hill estate. This photograph taken from Lunham Road shows Burlington House, 2 Hawke Road, on the right.

Two Edwardian views of Crown Hill, which since 1939 has been known, ludicrously, as Crown Dale. The top picture was taken from Crown Point, and shows on the right the front gardens of the four Grecian Cottages in Crown Hill, of which the last two were demolished in 1998. The lower photograph was taken halfway down the hill, and looks across the valley to the original 1857 range of the convent and the twin water towers of the Crystal Palace. The nearest building on the left was part of the Lambeth Industrial Schools (see p. 94). On the right is St Wilfrid's Cottage, now 82 Crown Dale, which was built in the 1850s on the convent estate. It was sometimes called the Convent Lodge, and later became the presbytery.

10

Gipsy Hill & Dulwich Wood

This snow scene was recorded by John Woodland Fullwood, who lived at 23 Farquhar Road during and just after the First World War. His photograph shows the big houses on the other side of Farquhar Road, probably nos 4, 6, 8, and so on. Some of these were destroyed during the Second World War, and the rest came down in the fatal 1960s.

Above: The view from the top of Gipsy Hill as it was in the early 1910s, and very much as it ever will be, I hope. The buildings on the right date from the 1850s. The nearest is Grosvenor House, no. 10, which had two spells as a Young Women's Christian Association hostel between 1885 and 1918. Beyond it is the old police station, now no. 10a, which was built in 1854 (architect Charles Reeves) and replaced by the Central Hill station in 1940.

The detached houses that cascade down the east side of Gipsy Hill were once standard Upper Norwood architecture, but the type has become more scarce and valuable during sixty years of destruction. This is Roseville, no. 11, as it looked in 1905, when occupied by the family of William Hayhoe. The house was built in the early 1870s.

Christ Church, Gipsy Hill, designed by John Giles, was built in 1866–7, but the landmark tower, its most notable feature, was not completed until 1889. This photograph of it was taken from Woodland Hill in about 1910: the interior view below probably dates from the 1920s. Christ Church was gutted by fire in 1982, and the site was largely cleared to make way for the new church, built in 1987. The tower happily survived the fire, and in 1997 it was converted into Norwood's most unusual house.

Gipsy Hill from the corner of George Street (now Cawnpore Street), *c.* 1910. The elaborate shop on the right was Thomas French's Crystal Palace Dairy at 72 and 74. It was built in the early years of the twentieth century. French had founded the business more modestly in the 1860s at the two little whitewashed cottages beyond. The pub in the centre of the picture, with the union jack flying, was the George IV. It closed in the mid-1930s and was demolished in 2000.

The view up Gipsy Hill from the station, *c.* 1912. Just to the left of centre can be seen the Gipsy Hill Hotel, which was built in the mid-1860s. It was intended to serve the large new middle-class community that sprung up in the immediate vicinity (in Victoria Road, Dulwich Wood, etc.) after the opening of Gipsy Hill station in 1856.

The meadow between Gipsy Hill and Dulwich Wood Avenue, one of Norwood's most pleasant features, was long used by Thomas French of the Crystal Palace dairy (see p. 82) to pasture his cows, and was sometimes known as French's Field. It was common to see cows herded up and down Gipsy Hill well into the twentieth century. The inevitable south tower of the Crystal Palace appears in this Edwardian photograph, and also in the one below, which was taken from the fork of Alleyn Road and Alleyn Park. It shows the gate piers of The Avenue. They do not survive, and The Avenue has been known as Dulwich Wood Avenue since 1939.

Dulwich Wood Avenue still features a number of fine houses, but far more have been demolished. A few were destroyed by bombing, but most have been the victims of postwar policy. Homedale, no. 44, survived until the 1960s, which was longer than most. It was built in the early 1860s and originally known as Belmont House. These postcards were issued when it was Miss Annie Henkel's school in the first fifteen years of the twentieth century. The one above shows the garden front. The cramped tennis court was at the side, in the angle of The Avenue and Dulwich Wood Park. Homedale later served as an auxiliary war hospital, as part of the Gipsy Hill Training College, and finally as a nurses' home.

Homedale's neighbours, also built in the early 1860s and both now demolished, are seen here in about 1920. No. 40 The Avenue (on the right) was Harps Oak or Kin Ching, which had a similar fate to Homedale, as part of the training college between the wars, and of the nurses' home until the 1960s. No. 42, Charlton House or Hurstfield, was replaced by the new central block of the nurses' home before 1951.

Everleigh, 5 Kingswood Road, or 'Drive' as it is now called, was built in the 1870s for the father of A.E.W. Mason, and the future best-selling novelist (1865–1948) lived here while attending Dulwich College. This photograph was taken in the early 1920s, when, despite the hockey sticks, the house had become Miss M. Bult's Bedford College of Dancing. Everleigh was demolished in the early 1950s, and the flats named Roundell House were built on the site.

First known as Mulnath, 1 Dulwich Wood Park was built in about 1870. In 1883 the new tenant George William Dodds gave it the name Ethelhurst, in memory of his daughter. It was the death of Ethel Dodds in Sydenham that had prompted the family's move to Dulwich Wood. When they left early in the twentieth century the name changed once more, to The Limes. The house, which is seen here during the Dodds years, was demolished *c.* 1960.

This view of Farquhar Road, taken *c.* 1912, shows the early 1870s houses, all now demolished, at the northern corner of Jasper Road. On the left is part of Belfort House, 59 Farquhar Road. No. 61, beyond, was built as a pair, but became the Ravenstone boarding house before 1880. The first tenants of the nearer half, which was called The Firs, were the Irish writers Samuel Carter Hall and Anna Maria Hall. Mrs Hall was a popular novelist in her day.

11

Gipsy Road & District

The photographer, probably in the summer of 1910, was standing on the slope of the Auckland Hill railway bridge, not far from the Gipsy Tavern, and looking along the central section of Gipsy Road towards the north tower of the Crystal Palace. The turning in the centre of the picture, by the lamppost, is St Gothard Road.

These two photographs of the Paxton Hotel and Tavern were taken when Benjamin George Stringer was the landlord, *c.* 1908. As the name suggests, this was one of the pubs built in the early 1850s to serve or exploit the visitors to Sir Joseph's masterpiece. In fact it appears to have been known for the first few years as the Palace Hotel and Tavern. In the background of the bottom picture can be seen the wooded hill that was shortly to become part of Norwood Park. At this time it was still the garden of Inglewood in Salters Hill.

The Gipsy Road Baptist chapel was built in 1881–2 and the lecture hall behind in 1890, both during the energetic and eventually controversial ministry of the Revd Walter Hobbs. The architect of both was Hampden W. Pratt. This photograph was taken in the 1930s, when the Revd Charles Lower was pastor.

As this photograph was taken in about 1908 it is surprising that such a crowd was attracted by what had become a common sight, but then Gipsy Road is rather boring, and no doubt any distraction was welcome. This is the view from Salters Hill towards Gipsy Hill past the Baptist chapel. The houses in the right foreground were approximately four years old at this time, but the four taller ones next to the chapel are twenty years older.

This 1920s photograph of Salters Hill shows the view down towards Central Hill, with Norwood Park on the right. Clayland Road was the original name, but Salters Hill had replaced it by the middle of the nineteenth century. The Salter family lived at Bloomfield (later known as Inglewood), the house that dominated the north-west side. Its site is now part of the park.

The Gipsy Road (now Norwood Park) Schools had their origin in the Chapel Road British (that is, non-conformist) schools, which were transferred to the School Board for London in 1872. A new building was opened in 1875. The architect was E.R. Robson, but all his work has vanished during various additions and alterations. The building in the foreground of this postcard, *c.* 1914, is the Junior Mixed School of 1895–6, designed by T.J. Bailey.

Zingari Villas was the delightful old name for 15 to 21 Gipsy Road, a terrace built in the mid-1870s. They survive in excellent condition. The two houses seen here in 1907 are nos 15 and 17, which were then occupied by James Chamberlain, a carpenter, and by Thomas Dunstone. Dunstone and Son, as the notice on their fanlight proclaims, were plumbers, gas, hot water and sanitary engineers, and house decorators.

Emmanuel Church, Clive Road, seen here in about 1907, was built in 1876–7, and lasted just ninety years. The architect of this and a number of other unremarkable churches in South London was E.C. Robins, who also designed Coombe Cliffe, the Horniman house at Croydon. It would be pleasant to be able to say that the new Emmanuel church is an improvement.

It is striking how often old photographs are found to have been taken from outside public houses. This view of Hamilton Road from the Bricklayers' Arms, which was probably captured in 1907, shows a scene that has not changed dramatically today, except of course for the cars. Hamilton Road is one of the pleasant surprises of West Norwood. A good proportion of the original 1850s cottages survive, and most are very well groomed.

12

Elder Road & Norwood High Street

A major contributor to the cost of Norwood Park (see p. 95) was Sir Ernest Tritton, MP for Norwood until 1906, who lived at Bloomfield Hall on the other side of Salter's Hill. The Bloomfield woods can be seen in the background of this photograph of *c.* 1914. In the foreground is the drinking fountain (now removed, of course), which was the gift of Sir Ernest and Lady Tritton.

Elder Road, *c.* 1907, showing the entrance to the old Lambeth Industrial Schools and the lodge built in 1887. Beyond it is the terrace known as Maudslay Cottages, built in the 1850s by Henry Maudslay of Holderness House, Knight's Hill, at the bottom of his garden. These survive except for no. 3, the whitewashed Park Tavern (now 54 and 56 Elder Road), which was rebuilt in the 1920s. The pub's advertising board is on the wall of the present no. 60.

The Lambeth House of Industry for the Infant Poor, the junior branch of the workhouse, was opened in Elder Road in 1810. It grew throughout the nineteenth century, most dramatically when Elder Lodge, a house to the north of the original site, was acquired. Huge new ranges of dormitories, designed by Edward Buckmaster Coe, were built over the garden in 1883–4. This was the main entrance in 1905. All these new buildings were demolished in about 1970.

There has been some exaggeration about the 'old' cottage in Norwood Park, for the 1806 enclosure map shows no buildings in this area. It had certainly appeared by the 1820s, when Henry Vincent, a nurseryman, lived there. This photograph was taken shortly before the land was bought as part of Norwood Park in 1908. The cottage was tidied up and retained as a storehouse after the park opened in 1911, but it perished in a fire in 1942.

This was the view from Chapel Road towards Gipsy Road, with the turnings to Norwood High Street on the left and to Elder Road on the right, *c.* 1918. With so many schools in Gipsy Road and Elder Road this was not the spot for those allergic to children. The trees on the right were in the garden of Clifton Lodge (formerly Morfa Lodge), a house probably built in the 1820s and demolished in 1947. Its garden stretched far down Gipsy Road.

Between 1913 and 1923 James Shield had his nursery garden in Elder Road, opposite the Lambeth Schools, and his shop here at 38 Chapel Road. It was part of a terrace of three houses probably built in the 1840s. They still survive, but no. 38 has been greatly altered, with the shop removed, the windows repositioned, and the ground in front excavated to create a semi-basement, so that the door is now approached by a flight of steps.

The Congregational Church, from which Chapel Road took its new name, after being originally part of Gipsy or Gipsy House Road, was opened in 1820. It is the oldest church in Norwood, and one of the oldest buildings. The wings were added after 1843, as schools. The one on the left in this Edwardian postcard was for boys, that on the right for infants. The girls' school was at the rear. The church is now used as a community centre.

Ernest Street (which became Ernest Avenue in 1938) was developed from the 1860s. It began as a short cul-de-sac branching off Norwood High Street, and took nearly thirty years to reach Knight's Hill. This is the view from the High Street end, *c.* 1909. The corner shops survive, but the first two houses on the right are the only original buildings still standing in Ernest Avenue itself, where the bus garage is now the main feature.

Tivoli Road was presumably named after the Tivoli pleasure gardens, which lay behind the King's Head in Norwood High Street. This photograph of *c.* 1910 shows the original northern end, from Dassett Road to Linton Grove, which was built between 1900 and 1904. Tivoli Road was extended south to Crown Hill in the early 1920s.

The honour of having been Norwood's first shopping centre belongs to Knight's Hill, but Norwood High Street had overtaken it by the 1830s, and retained the lead in West Norwood until the 1880s. This 1920s photograph of the High Street shows the view south towards Elder Road, with the King's Head, no. 82, on the right. This was one of the district's oldest pubs. It was founded in the 1820s, but probably rebuilt as seen here in about 1890.

The High Street seen from the up platform of West Norwood station in the early 1930s. On the left is the Hope, which seems to have been founded in the late 1830s. Most of Norwood's old pubs have been rebuilt, but the Hope is still happily flourishing in the original premises.

13

Knight's Hill & the Streatham Borders

The British Home and Hospital for Incurables, which had been founded at Clapham in 1861, moved to Crown Lane in 1894. The new home (built on the site of a house called Norwood Lodge) was designed by Arthur Cawston, who was killed in a shooting accident only a few weeks before the opening ceremony. There have been several extensions since the 1890s, the most recent in 1996. This postcard was sent in 1910.

The striking and depressing fact about this 1920s aerial view of Streatham Common North Side is that not one of the twelve elaborate and expensive houses shown is still standing. A couple were destroyed in the war, but most were pulled down by Lambeth Council in 1951–2. The most regrettable loss is perhaps the house in the right foreground. This was Redroofs, Ryecroft Road, which Sir Ernest George, Norwood's most distinguished architect, built for himself in the late 1880s. It was bombed in 1941. The large mid 1880s mansion at the corner of Ryecroft Road and Streatham Common was Jerviston House. At the other corner of Ryecroft Road (top right) can be seen part of Redclyffe, Crown Lane, the only other house on the Croydon side of the road. It was built *c.* 1905. The nine houses on the Lambeth portion of Streatham Common North Side, between Leigham Court Road and Crown Lane, were, from left to right, Fern Lodge and Oak Lodge (a semi-detached pair), White Lodge, Gresham Lodge, Warrington Lodge, South Hill, Esam Lodge, Winton Lodge, and Hill House. Winton Lodge was originally semi-detached, but by the 1920s Sir Herbert Parsons, managing director of Phosferine Ltd, had incorporated Charnwood, the smaller section, into his enlarged house. Sir Herbert died at Winton Lodge in 1940. All these fine houses on the Lambeth side were built in the 1820s and '30s. The one with the most interesting residents was Hill House, which from the 1820s to the 1860s was the home of Thomas Griffith, the agent for the sale of J.M.W. Turner's paintings and drawings – which meant that Turner was a frequent visitor. The eminent judge Sir John Hamilton, Lord Sumner, was a later resident. He lived here in the early years of the twentieth century, when the house was known as Crown Lane End. How much open land there still was in this part of Upper Norwood! Streatham Common (bottom left) remains today, of course, but the large gardens of Jerviston House and of the Streatham Common North Side houses have all been built over, as has the ground on the right edge of the picture, in the loop of Ryecroft Road.

Opposite: Rosslyn School was the name for 105 St Julian's Farm Road from 1925 until the 1940s, when Mrs Alexander Bothwell ran it as a day school for girls, with a preparatory department for boys, and a kindergarten. The photograph was taken during that period. The house was built in the mid-1890s, and known at first as Thurlby. It was converted into flats in 1987.

St Julian's Farm Road began as a track leading to the farmhouse, which stood at the point where Thornlaw Road now crosses, and continued as a footpath to Streatham. Early in the nineteenth century there were plans to promote it into a road, as part of an abortive scheme for the development of the Thurlow estate, but it had to wait until the 1880s to get beyond the footpath stage. This Edwardian view down the hill from Thurlestone Road features houses of the 1890s.

St Julian's College, 62 Wolfington Road, seen here in 1911, was built *c.* 1900, and for the first fourteen years run as a girls' school by Mrs Henrietta Mary Newbery. It then became a private house, as it has remained.

Thornlaw House, 128 Thornlaw Road, was looking rather attractive when this publicity shot was taken from the garden in 1906. It still survives, but is now half hidden from the road, behind some very ugly garages. Thornlaw House was built in about 1890, and ten years later became the West Norwood Nursing Home, which was run by the Misses Tyrell until the early 1920s.

At the corner of Knight's Hill and Crown Dale, where since the 1940s there has been only a forlorn patch of windswept grass, stood some of the oldest shops in Norwood. They were known as Clifford Place. This picture shows the last three shops in Knight's Hill in 1909. From 1830 they had been occupied as one property by Thomas Blunden, a grocer and fishmonger. He later ran a beershop here as well, and his widow added the duties of postmistress. The large Blunden shop was sub-divided in the 1850s. In 1909 the three parts were William Hodder's greengrocery at no. 235, Richard Stanford's Knight's Hill Cigar Stores at no. 237, and the house of Richard Ottewell, a carman (removals contractor, etc.) at no. 239. There is a later photograph of these shops in Jill Dudman's *Brixton and Norwood*, p. 106.

The view down Knight's Hill *c.* 1904, with the West Norwood Wesleyan Church on the right. It was built in 1852–3. The congregation dispersed in the 1970s, and the church lay derelict for years before being demolished in about 1989. The block of flats built on the site in the mid-1990s is called, in a fine flight of inspiration, Church Court. The houses on the right, 5 to 3 Brunswick Place, shared the fate of their neighbour.

This view of Chapel Road from Knight's Hill, *c.* 1910, gives a good view of Norwood Technical Institute. It was built in 1858–9 as the Lower Norwood Working Men's Institute, and paid for by Arthur Anderson of Norwood Grove, the chairman of the P&O line. His architect was the Gothic eccentric Edward Buckton Lamb. The old building was demolished in the early 1970s to make way for the large glass and concrete block that has now (unlamented) met the same fate.

One of the many fine buildings (worth all their tribe) that the rulers of Norwood have thrown away in the last fifty years is the Jews' Hospital and Orphan Asylum, which is seen here in the early 1900s. The narrow entrance opposite the station in Knight's Hill gave no clue to the splendour waiting around the corner. The orphanage was designed by Tillott and Chamberlain in imitation of a Jacobean manor house, and built between 1861 and 1863. Sadly, the children were evacuated in 1939, and never returned, and the main building was demolished in about 1960. Only the lodge of 1862, now 38 Knight's Hill, survives from that period.

The old West Norwood public library in Knight's Hill, a pathetic object since its replacement by the cemetery library, was built in 1887–8, to designs by Sidney R.J. Smith. The site was given by Frederick Nettlefold of Norwood Grove, a house that inspired its owners with charitable thoughts. In 1936 an extension to the library replaced the shop seen in the foreground of this photograph, *c.* 1910. The building beyond the library was the postal sorting office.

St Luke's Church, seen here from the Knight's Hill gates, *c.* 1910, was built between 1822 and 1825. The grand portico was the best feature of Francis Bedford's design; but unfortunately, while the site dictated that the church should face the north, canon law laid down that the altar must face the east, so that the magnificent entrance led to a very muddled interior. The solution was not found until the 1870s.

Below: There is a sharp contrast between the classical exterior of St Luke's, and the Romanesque interior imposed upon it by George Edmund Street (of Law Courts fame) in 1871–2. This photograph of *c.* 1910 shows the church largely as Street left it, although several other men, including John F. Bentley, the architect of Westminster Cathedral, made additions in the 1880s.

14

Norwood Road & the Dulwich Borders

Norwood Road was residential until the 1870s, the only rows of shops south of the railway bridge being next to the Thurlow Arms and on the corners of Lansdowne Hill. One of the first changes was the building of the parade between Chestnut Road and Chatsworth Road (seen on the right of this photograph, *c.* 1918) in the early 1880s. The Broadway, the great row of shops beyond Chatsworth Road, completed the transformation ten years later.

The South Metropolitan Cemetery, which opened in 1837, was one of the burial businesses established after 1832 to relieve the strain on London's churchyards. Sir William Tite's layout and the buildings he designed gave the cemetery and West Norwood some architectural distinction, but all except his stone gateway (seen here just before the First World War) have been wantonly destroyed. The lodge was demolished in 1936, no doubt as a centenary celebration.

West Norwood is fortunate in having a memorable town centre, with the division of Norwood Road into Knight's Hill and the High Street dramatically marked by the portico and tower of St Luke's. The bustling scene, a favourite with postcard publishers, is captured here from Knight's Hill in about 1910. Today the motor car, which spoils so much, has turned this from a place of pleasure into one of danger.

Lansdowne Hill, which was known as Sydenham Grove until 1869, was laid out in the late 1830s. The development was on quite an ambitious scale, but the railway blighted the road in 1856. Five houses had to be demolished, and all the other original buildings have gone since. Some still survived on the north side (the left) when this photograph was taken from the railway bridge, *c.* 1910. The terrace on the right was built in the 1880s.

The strong personalities that abounded in Norwood non-conformist circles ensured that there were many quarrels and schisms. After fourteen years as minister of the Chatsworth Road Baptist Church (see p. 110), William Fuller Gooch left in 1892 to rally a Free Evangelical congregation. This iron church in Lansdowne Hill was built for it in 1893, and the lecture hall on the right in 1897. That survives, but the church was retired to Clacton in 1906, when work began on the present building. The Norwood Road shops on the left have been replaced by the little supermarket at the corner of Chestnut Road. (*Ron Elam*)

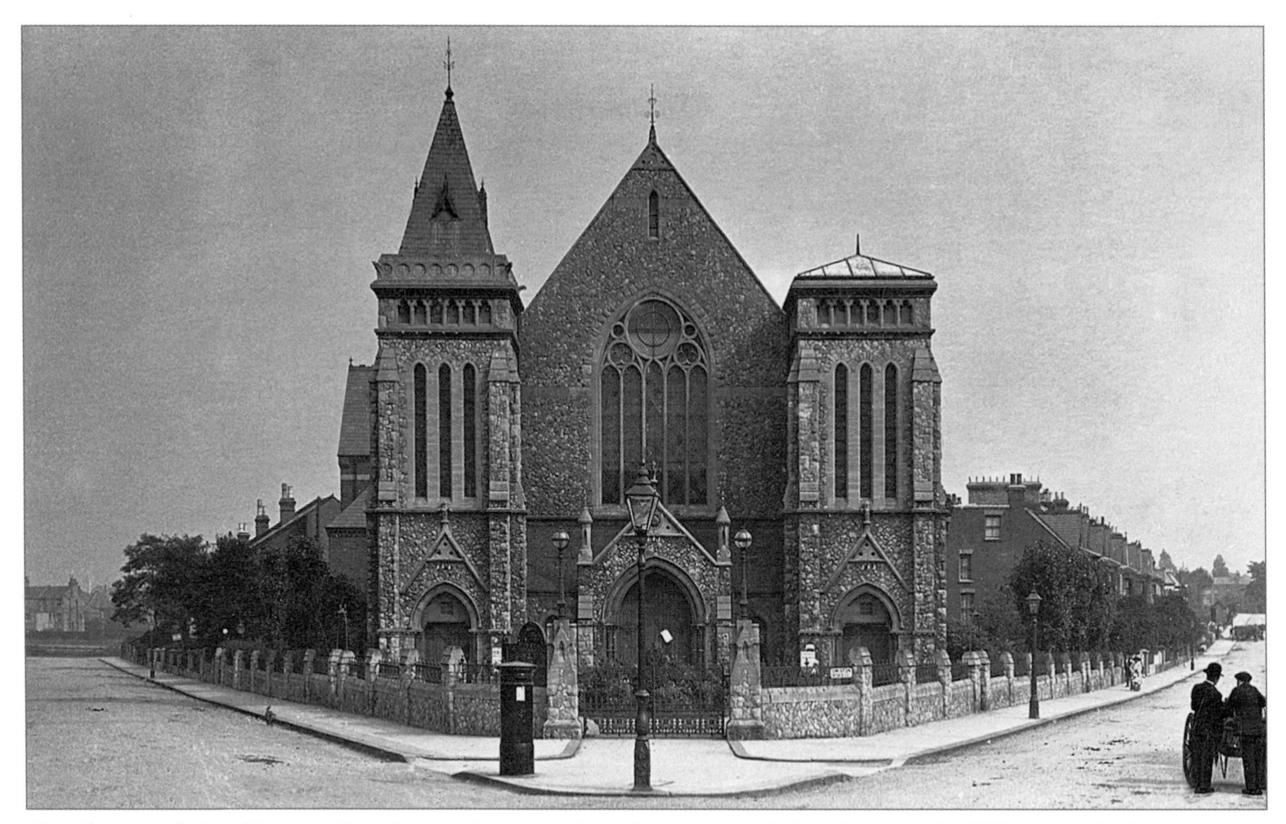

The Chatsworth Road Baptist Church, seen here outside and in as it was before the First World War, was built in 1876–7. It was large and expensive, to suit the prosperous congregation of these West Dulwich border lands. One of the architects was Edward Power, who is also credited with the Presbyterian church (now Greek Orthodox) in Westow Street. In 1900 an equally lavish Sunday School was built behind the church. But it was labour in vain, for in 1944 all the complex except for the two towers was levelled in an instant by a V2 rocket. The church has been rebuilt in a very different style.

Lancaster Avenue, one of the most attractive roads in Norwood, was originally suggested in the 1840s. The first four houses were built in the '50s, and the oldest of them, Prairie House, still survives as no. 16. It was occupied by 1855. 'Avenue' is one of the London County Council's many changes: the name was Lancaster Road until 1936. This Edwardian view from the Norwood Road end shows nos 5, 7, 9, etc. on the left.

For all its modern popularity Lancaster Avenue was not a runaway success at first. In fact it took fifty years to complete, with the section between Ardlui Road and Thurlow Park Road only being built *c.* 1905. The larger pairs opposite these latecomers date from the early 1880s. This example is Oakfield, no. 45, as it looked in 1910, when it was occupied by Miss E. Dunn. It survives in excellent condition.

Thurlow Lodge, 431 Norwood Road, could not have been the home of Lord Chancellor Thurlow, as is sometimes stated, for it was built between his death (in 1806) and 1824. The true great resident was Sir Hiram Maxim (see p. 65), who lived here on and off between 1887 and 1913. The lady in the doorway in this Edwardian view is identified as Grace Simmonds. Serbia House, as it was called after Maxim's day, was demolished in the mid-1960s.

An Edwardian postcard of Elmcourt Road, showing the view towards Norwood Road. The 'to be sold' board was perhaps outside no. 18, which was the home of Arthur Mee, the writer for children, from 1902 to 1905. Elmcourt Road, of which the first houses were built in 1870–1, was known as Court Road until 1926. The new name came from Elmcourt, no. 22, a large house that became a London County Council home for blind children.

This sunny view of Norwood Road was taken shortly before the First World War from nearly opposite Avenue Park Road. The turning to the left in the centre of the picture is Court (now Elmcourt) Road. The signboard belonged to the West Norwood Constitutional, or Conservative, Club, which had its headquarters at The Elms from *c.* 1887 to 1914. This house was built in the 1850s and demolished in about 1930.

Sibton House was one of several names used for 395 Norwood Road, which is seen here after it had abandoned such vanities. It was one of a trio of villas built in the 1850s between Avenue Park Road, on the left, and Elmcourt Road. Another, Bervie House, is glimpsed on the right. The Elms was the third. By 1911 Sibton House was divided into offices occupied by surveyors, a solicitor, a typist, etc., and the coach house had become a paper shop. Bervie House was demolished in about 1930: Sibton House was wrecked by a flying bomb in 1944. (*Ron Elam*)

Tulsemere Road, which was built between 1906 and 1912 (the likely date of this picture), has no claim to architectural distinction, but despite the tameness of its houses it still has a very dramatic effect when seen, as here, from Idmiston Road. Its straight course across the little valley south of Lancaster Road leads directly to the former Dulwich High School, with an effect far more startling to the eye than the lens can ever capture.

The Dulwich High School at 70 Thurlow Park Road was notable as one of the failures of the Girls' Public Day School Company. The building dates from 1870 and was intended as a private house. There were no takers, and the High School occupied it from 1878 until 1913, when state competition proved its ruin. Other institutions, including the Old Vic Theatre School, have come and gone, but since 1976 this has been the Rosemead Preparatory School.

The junction of Court (now Elmcourt) Road and Thurlow Park Road, seen from Court Road, *c.* 1908. The houses in the centre (nos 59, 61, etc. Thurlow Park Road) were then new. Lovelace Road, in the distance, was originally part of Court Road, or distinguished as Upper Court Road. On the right is St Cuthbert's Presbyterian Church, which was built on the site of a temporary iron structure, from the designs of Arthur Owen Breeds, in 1900. It is now a children's nursery.

The southern side of Thurlow Park Road in the Dalmore Road area was one of the last sections to be developed. Mamore, no. 80, which was built in about 1890, is the most prominent house in this group. It is seen here before the First World War, when a Miss Dolphin was the occupant. During the war it became the West Dulwich (later Thurlow Park) Nursing Home, and it was used for the same purpose until quite recently. Mamore is now divided into flats.

Except for the section south of Park Hall Road, Rosendale Road was planned in the 1840s, like others on the Thurlow Park estate, and laid out in the 1850s. There were some eight houses, plus the Rosendale Hotel, by 1860. This view, *c.* 1908, from Thurlow Park Road shows on the left no. 170 (Devonia Lodge, later Glenarm Lodge), which was built in the 1870s. It looks rather different now because the parapet has been unwisely removed.

The view along Park, or Park Hall, Road towards the Rosendale Hotel, with part of the attractive Thurlow Villas (built 1850–1) on the right. The date is *c.* 1912. This was the oldest section of the road, for it was originally a drive leading from Croxted Lane to Rosendale Hall. The first scheme for making it the southern artery of the Thurlow Park estate involved extending it along the line of Chestnut Road, but the creation of the cemetery in 1837 moved it south to the present Robson Road, which was part of Park Road until 1903.

15

Tulse Hill & Environs

A lively scene at Norwood Road's junction with Tulse Hill and Thurlow Park Road, *c.* 1912. The clock belonged to Mervyn Philcox, whose long-enduring watchmaker's business was at no. 108 (now no. 160). It has been said that the Tulse Hill Hotel was built in 1840, but a market gardener's house was on the site by 1824. The pub was founded in the 1840s. The shops beyond it were built in the late 1870s, and originally called Romola Terrace.

Tulse Hill station and what is now Station Rise seen from Norwood Road, *c.* 1908, when Harold Norton was landlord of the White Hart Tavern. The road was part of Maley Avenue until the railway cut them in two in 1868. It was then known as Tulse Hill Station Road for a couple of years, and as Approach Road until 1937. The buildings are all of the late 1860s or early '70s.

This reverse view was taken from one of the station windows, *c.* 1916. The clock in both pictures belonged to Frederick Lockwood, the watchmaker at no. 6. The Methodist church (see p. 119) dominated the area. Even the most militantly atheist commuter, emerging exhausted from the station, would surely rather see this than the peculiarly ugly shops that have replaced the church and its elegant carriage sweep.

The delicate landmark spire of the Roupell Park Wesleyan church, Norwood Road, seen from Christchurch Road, *c*. 1911. It was designed by Charles Bell and built in 1879–80. Following the Norwood Methodist tradition the prime part of the site was surrendered to a supermarket in 1969, and the replacement Centre 70 church was built behind in Christchurch Road.

This domestic scene was recorded in the garden of Osborne Lodge, 181 Tulse Hill, in the summer of 1909. The postcard was sent to her grandmother by the maid, who reported that 'this is a photo of mistress and I'. 'I' was named Daisy, possibly Daisy Wilson, and 'mistress' was perhaps Mrs Powell. The dog remains anonymous. The house was built in the 1850s, and demolished in about 1970. Parts of Poullett and Coppin Houses are on the site.

Tulse Hill is one of south London's architectural disasters. Some 160 villas, mostly detached, were built here between 1820 and 1890. They included good specimens of suburban architecture from all those dates, but the ones from the earlier decades were particularly fine and plentiful. The survivors can now be counted on one hand. They do not include the two houses seen in this *c.* 1910 view up the hill from near the Norwood end.

It might have been called the original St Luke's vicarage, except that the first ministers were curates. The house was Hill Crest, 124 Tulse Hill, which was built in 1825, and probably occupied immediately by the Rev. Arthur Gibson, who was appointed to St Luke's in that year. This card was sent in 1907 by the Bone family. Hill Crest was cobbled into flats as Hillcrest Court in the 1930s, but even in that form did not last much longer. Harbin House is now on the site.

This was the lull before the storm. Although well past its prime, Tulse Hill was still looking very properous on this sunny day in the early 1930s; but destruction from wartime bombs and post-war policy was imminent. Tulse Hill is in the bottom left of the picture, with Deronda Road bottom right. Trinity Rise runs across the top half of the view, with Brockwell Park Gardens beyond and Brockwell Park itself in the far distance. Holy Trinity Church (see p. 126) is a prominent object, with the old vicarage, now demolished, to its right. The large white building in Tulse Hill is the St Martin-in-the-Fields High School for Girls, which acquired this new site in 1913 and moved here from the Charing Cross Road in 1928. Its new home was Silwood Hall (formerly Berry House), which had been built in 1856/7. It is the only surviving building in this part of Tulse Hill, and that survival has only been a matter of chance. The school authorities intended to demolish Silwood Hall, but successive rebuilding plans were frustrated by the First World War and postwar austerity, and the cheaper alternative of adding to the house was adopted. In the 1930s the extensive playing fields ran down to the grounds of the Westmorland Society's School in Norwood Road. The large houses on either side of the St Martin-in-the-Fields School were Egremont Lodge (no. 153) to the left, and Kenilworth (no. 157) to the right. Egremont Lodge was built in 1853, and Kenilworth, which was the last of the original Tulse Hill houses, in 1888.

This is the crest of Tulse Hill, where the climb from Norwood becomes the descent into Brixton. On the left is the entrance to Upper Tulse Hill, and on the right to Trinity Road, which has been known as Trinity Rise since 1914. One of the policemen standing by the fire alarm at the corner is unfortunately hiding all but the 'R' of 'Road' or 'Rise', but the photograph was almost certainly taken a few years before 1914.

Here is a close companion piece to the photograph above, as it looks towards the same junction from the direction of Upper Tulse Hill. The spire of Holy Trinity Church, Trinity Road (see p. 126), can be faintly seen in the distance. The date is *c.* 1910, since when this scene has been utterly transformed.

The curious novel estate in the angle between Norwood Road and Tulse Hill was laid out in the late 1870s and built during the 1880s. These two Edwardian postcards give a good idea of the style of development. The one above shows the view down Deronda Road, with Deerbrook Road on the right, and Norwood Road in the distance. (George Eliot's *Daniel Deronda* was published in 1876, and Harriet Martineau's *Deerbrook* in 1839.) The bottom picture is of Deerbrook Road, again looking down the hill towards Norwood Road. The man up the ladder on the left was painting 15 Berwyn Road.

Madame H.E. Angless's Pompadour Ladies' Orchestra was a far cry from Sweet Sue and Her Society Syncopators, but several of the musicians do look suspiciously like men in drag. Emily Angless, seen here with the baton, taught music at 76 Norwood Road (now no. 126) during the first decade of the twentieth century, but her orchestra was known much farther afield. She sent this card to a young aspirant in Scarborough to explain that she had 'no vacancy just now'.

The development of the east side of Norwood Road to the north of St Faith's Road must have been hampered by the close proximity of the railway line; yet the best group of houses was built where the plots were smallest, presumably because the wider garden of a double-fronted house compensated for its shortness. The four in the foreground of this *c.* 1910 view are nos 277 to 271, known as York House, Gilling Lodge, Kerton (or Broughton) Lodge, and Gordon (or Llanberis) Lodge. York House was built in the 1880s, the other three in the early 1870s. All are still standing.

Trinity Road, known since 1914 as Trinity Rise, owes its existence to Holy Trinity Church (see p. 126), which was built in 1855–6. A possible pre-history is hinted at by the fact that Ashurst Lodge, the house at the corner of Tulse Hill, was built in the mid-nineteenth century. It is seen on the right of the very early twentieth-century postcard above. But Ashurst Lodge was included in Tulse Hill in 1850s lists, and may have been built before Trinity Road, or much of it, existed. It was unusual in being occupied throughout its brief career – it was demolished in about 1910 – by members of the Howis family, who were oilmen to Queen Victoria. A few houses were built close to the church in the 1860s, but the south side of Trinity Road was not completed to the Norwood Road end until the 1880s. As the Edwardian view below indicates, the north side remained open until *c.* 1910.

Holy Trinity was built in 1855–6 on a site provided by the owner of the Tulse Hill estate, and largely at his expense. A church was the finishing touch to any ambitious Victorian development. Such a gift could hardly be refused, so the Church Building Commissioners ignored the agonised complaints of the vicar of St Luke's. He lost the wealthiest members of his congregation, and their pew rents, to the new parish, and the great St Luke's crisis of the 1860s was the result. Holy Trinity (seen here inside and out in about 1907) was designed by Thomas Denville Barry of Liverpool. It survives in good condition, though the three stained glass windows in the apse were destroyed during the Second World War. They were replaced in 1951. The building in front of the church was the gardener's cottage of Ashhurst Lodge (see p. 125).

Index to Main Subjects